SOUND

Troll Associates

SOUND

by Keith Brandt

Illustrated by Lynn Sweat

Troll Associates

Library of Congress Cataloging in Publication Data

Brandt, Keith, (date)
   Sound.

   Summary: Discusses what a sound is, how sounds are
made by musical instruments and the human voice, sound
in a vacuum, and the speed of sound.
   1. Sound—Juvenile literature. [1. Sound] I. Sweat,
Lynn, ill.   II. Title.
QC225.5.B69   1984   534   84-2632
ISBN 0-8167-0128-8 (lib. bdg.)
ISBN 0-8167-0129-6 (pbk.)

Day and night you hear sounds...the voices of your parents, your teacher, your friends. You hear a radio, a television set, or a record player. You hear a fire engine, a car horn, a truck rumbling down the street. You hear a dog barking, a bird singing, a rooster crowing. No matter where you are, you hear sounds.

8

What exactly is sound? Sound is the result of a certain kind of movement called *vibration*. Vibration is a very fast, back-and-forth movement. Sometimes you can see the kind of vibration that makes sound.

Did you ever stretch a rubber band until it was very tight, and then pluck it with your fingers? If you did, you saw it move back and forth. At first it moved very fast, then it got slower and slower until it stopped. While it was moving you heard it *twang*, then *hum*, until it stopped vibrating.

You can feel vibrations, too. Put your hand on the front of your neck. Now hum a song or say a few words. At the same time that you hear the sound of your voice, you will feel the vibrations making it. You can also feel sound vibrations by touching the top of a radio while it is on, or by putting a finger on a drum while someone is playing it.

Even when we don't see or feel sound vibrations, we can still hear the sound. Imagine a bell being rung in the next room. The bar inside the bell is swinging back and forth, hitting the sides of the bell. The bell vibrates.

As this happens, the air inside and around the bell is being squeezed. The squeezed air

moves away from the bell to where it will have more space. It moves at a steady rate of speed. In other words, it vibrates.

This vibration of the air moves further and further away, like the ripples made by a pebble dropped into a pond. When the vibration reaches your ear, you hear the bell ringing.

Sounds vibrate at different speeds. A high sound—like the song of a bird—is made up of very fast vibrations that come from the bird's throat. A low sound—like the *oom-pah* of a big tuba—is made up of slower vibrations that come from inside that musical instrument.

The number of sound vibrations produced in one second is the *frequency* of the sound. High sounds have a high frequency. Low sounds have a low frequency.

Musicians use a word to describe the frequencies of sound made by their instruments. The word is *pitch*. A tuba sends out low-pitched sounds. A flute sends out high-pitched sounds. A piano can produce high-pitched notes, low-pitched notes, and all the notes in between.

A rubber band that is stretched very tightly vibrates at a very high frequency. So the sound it makes has a high pitch. If you loosen the rubber band a bit, it vibrates at a lower frequency than before. And the sound it makes has a lower pitch.

There are many musical instruments that make sounds the same way that plucking a rubber band does. These are called string instruments. The guitar and the harp are two string instruments.

Other musical instruments produce sounds when air is forced through them. These are called wind instruments. The tuba, the trumpet, and the slide trombone are three wind instruments.

Still other instruments make sounds when they are hit. These are called percussion instruments. The drum and the cymbal are two percussion instruments.

There is an instrument we all have that uses a combination of wind and strings. This marvelous instrument is the human voice. In your throat are a pair of thick bands called vocal cords. When you speak or sing, these cords are vibrated and produce the sound that is your voice. In that way your voice is like a string instrument.

But what makes your vocal cords vibrate? Air, pushed out of your lungs, past the vocal cords. In that way your voice is like a wind instrument. Push just a little air out of your lungs, and your voice will be very quiet. Push a lot of air out of your lungs, and your voice will be very loud.

You can make your voice do lots of things...squeak like a mouse, moo like a cow, and hiss like a snake. And you can change the pitch of your voice from one moment to the next. You do it every time you sing a song.

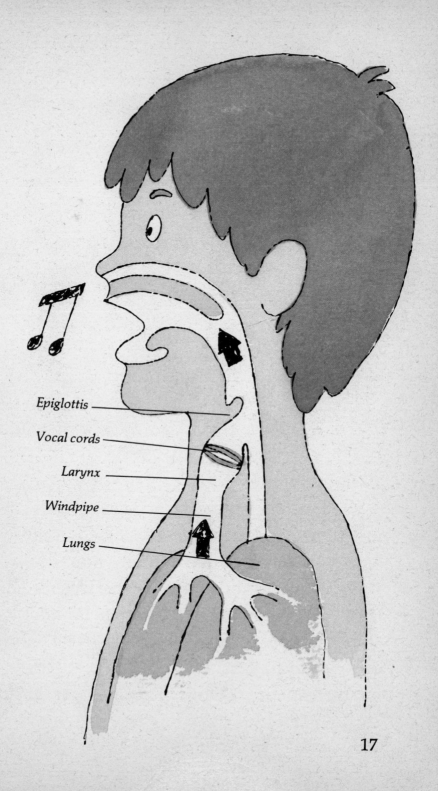

Epiglottis

Vocal cords

Larynx

Windpipe

Lungs

17

We hear the sound of a voice, a musical instrument, or the ringing of a bell because sound travels through the air. Sound also travels through other things, besides air. It travels through water and other liquids. It travels through metals, wood, stone, and other solid objects.

You can prove this. Tap a finger very

lightly on a tabletop. If the room is quiet, you'll hear the light tapping. If the room is noisy, you probably won't hear the tapping at all. Now press an ear against the table and tap just as lightly as before. You'll hear the tapping much better, whether the room is quiet or noisy. That's because sound travels better through a solid than through air.

In a vacuum, where there is no solid, liquid, or gas (such as air), there is no sound at all. Long ago an English scientist named Robert Boyle proved this. He put a ticking watch inside a glass jar and sealed the jar. He could still hear the watch ticking.

Then he pumped the air out of the jar, and the ticking grew fainter and fainter. When all the air was out, there was no ticking sound, even though the watch was still running.

Then Robert Boyle began to let air back into the jar—and the ticking grew louder and louder. This experiment proved that sound is carried through the air, and that there is no sound in a vacuum.

Why is there no sound in a vacuum? Because all sound is made by vibrations called sound waves, and in a vacuum there is no air to carry the vibrations.

Sound waves move fast. That's why you hear a ball bounce on the ground at just about the same time you bounce it. But sound doesn't travel as fast as light.

During a thunderstorm you see the jagged flash of lightning in the sky. Seconds later you hear the booming thunder, which is the sound the lightning makes. The farther away the lightning is, the longer it takes between the time you see the lightning and the time you hear the thunder.

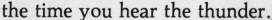

Sound waves can be reflected, or bounced back. Imagine you are standing in a valley and facing a far-off mountain wall. You shout "Hel-looo!" and a few moments later you hear "Hel-looo!" It is the echo of your voice.

The sound waves of your voice were reflected off the mountain and returned to you. All echoes are made this way: sound travels a distance, hits a surface, and reflects back. Since we know how fast sound travels, we can use reflected sound waves to measure distances.

Sonar uses very, very high-frequency sound waves to measure the depth of the ocean. These waves are called ultrasonic sound, or ultrasound. They are so high that humans cannot hear them.

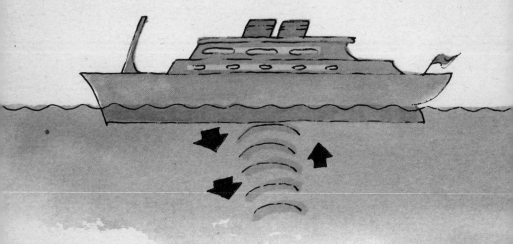

A ship with a sonar unit sends out ultrasonic waves, and records the time it takes for them to reach the ocean floor and bounce back. Then the sonar unit figures out the distance the sounds have traveled.

Animals also use ultrasound. Bats send out ultrasonic waves. When the waves hit something and echo back, the bats know they are near a solid object, like a tree or a wall. Dolphins also use ultrasound in water the way bats do in the air.

While humans cannot hear ultrasound, we can hear a very wide range of sounds. When sound waves enter our ears, they hit a thin, tight piece of skin called the eardrum. The eardrum vibrates, sending the sound waves through the bones and tunnels of the inner ear. Then the waves go to the brain, where they are changed into sounds we hear and understand.

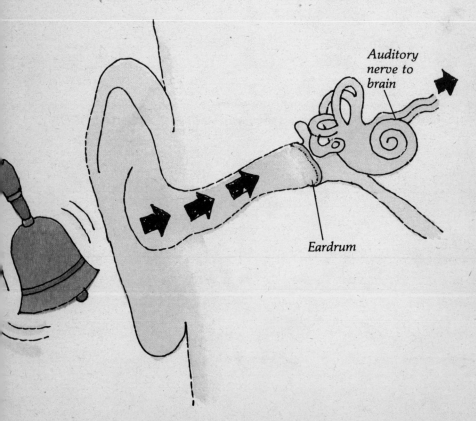

Auditory nerve to brain

Eardrum

The human ear is a remarkable thing. It can hear all kinds of sounds, from the softest whisper to the loudest boom. But there is one thing it cannot do. It cannot make a permanent record of what it hears. For that we need something like a phonograph record or a tape recording.

A little more than 100 years ago, the first recording machine was invented. It was made of a roll of soft metal and a tube with a vibrating top and a needle. Thomas Edison, the inventor, spoke into the tube while he turned the metal roll. The needle on the tube vibrated to the sound of his voice, making grooves in the metal roll. It was the first recorded sound—another miracle in our fantastic world of sound!